ETERNITY'S ESSENTIALS
POETIC
EVANGELISM

WILLIAM R. LAVELL

WESTBOW
PRESS®
A DIVISION OF THOMAS NELSON
& ZONDERVAN

Scripture quotations are taken from the King James Version of the Bible.

WestBow Press books may be ordered through booksellers or by contacting:

WestBow Press
A Division of Thomas Nelson & Zondervan
1663 Liberty Drive
Bloomington, IN 47403
www.westbowpress.com
1 (866) 928-1240

ISBN: 978-1-5127-6916-6 (sc)
ISBN: 978-1-5127-6917-3 (hc)
ISBN: 978-1-5127-6915-9 (e)

Library of Congress Control Number: 2016921041

Print information available on the last page.

WestBow Press rev. date: 1/16/2017

Contents

Acknowledgments

When I asked God how I may share the whispers of His will with this present generation and generations to come, He rekindled my love for poetry.

Early in life, when I was a young man and young father, poetry found my heart sharing love letters of prayers and poetry with my heavenly Father.

At some point, after a few years, life got busy, and the novelty of poetry seemed to fall by the wayside.

However, God has strongly renewed this passion in the last five years.

Many of the poems I have written stem from life lessons learned over my few decades of temporal living upon this earth.

I believe I obtained these pearls and nuggets from heaven to prepare me for when this temporal part of my journey on earth is over and my eternal journey begins.

Since God's truth pearls, which came from heaven, have been such a blessing and benefit to myself, God has convinced me to share His wonderful wisdom with all who have turned an ear toward His will.

I'm convinced that sharing God's truths worldwide will indeed benefit others as much as they have certainly benefited me.

I pray that the poetry comforts, challenges, and inspires hearts to a deeper and more intimate relationship with Almighty God, obtaining and maintaining a pathway of peace.

All glory be to my precious Savior, Jesus Christ of Nazareth.

In addition, I would like to give special thanks to the Holy Spirit, in whom all wisdom originates and of whom I'm privileged to be a sharing steward, with great thanks I'm eternally grateful for your inspiration.

Furthermore, thanks to my mother, whom I love dearly and eternally, as well as my family, who graciously sacrificed time that we would have otherwise cherished together.

Thanks to your love and support, I'm able to get this book's poetic messages of evangelism out to the church and the public.

Special thanks, as always, to West Bow Press, whose professionalism, encouragement, and support go beyond a mile.

Finally, my greatest desire is to thank my Lord God Almighty for His unfailing love, grace, and mercy.

Introduction

This book of poetry is dedicated to all disciples, evangelists, and martyrs who have devoted so much toward caring for those from whom time has stolen all hope, will and stamina to help themselves.

May we, by God's grace, continue to go to them.

Life has promised to be filled with persecutions, trials, tribulations, and hardships as well as joy, peace, freedom, and abundance.

Life, reality as we know it, demonstrates a balance of both joys and sorrows.

We are told to weep with those who weep and to rejoice with those who rejoice.

Yet God has promised to see us through everything; we will overcome and be more than conquerors, as He has promised to be with us.

God will see us through hardships, raging waters and the enemy's roars will not overtake us.

Look how far we have already come, after many trials, tests, and storms.

We still press on toward maturity in Christ.

We mature to become steady eddies of God's grace, pillars of calm in storms.

With experience, we endure and trust that the storms will pass by, having faith in God and with great patience we always are enabled to be more patient than the devil.

As we learn to endure and mature, God will always bring us back to His will so we can reach out with His life-preserving word out to those still lost and struggling in the storms of life, leaving none behind.

As instruments of God's peace, we will show to the world His love, which endures and reins forever.

I have composed a variety of heartfelt poems that God has inspired me to write.

There are many essentials on earth that we must acquire to prepare us for our eternal journey. Here are just a few that are expressed throughout this book.

- Honoring one's mother and father
- Taking personal responsibility for one's misfortunes without blaming others and doing an honest, balanced inventory of one's life
- Forgiving oneself and others
- Getting involved in some form of outreach evangelism, spreading the great news of God's saving grace and

redeeming power through His Loving Son, Jesus Christ of Nazareth

I believe wholeheartedly that these poetic messages reflect God's heartbeat and His wonderful desire for all peoples to be reconciled to Him.

God's greatest hope for us all is to know the joy of His steadfast love and intimacy.

Once we experience just the slightest taste and touch of His intimacy, it becomes so contagious that it compels us to share His grace and love with others.

I hope and pray that these poems stir up the treasures deep within your heart so that you can reach out to those who are destitute depressed in darkness and despair co-working with the precious Holy Spirit.

As sons and daughters of the one true illuminating light of Almighty God, we can brighten up people's lives every day and watch their darkness fade away.

Eternally In His Service
William R Lavell

Luke 4:18: The Spirit of the Lord is upon me,
because he hath anointed me to preach the gospel to the poor;
he hath sent me to heal the brokenhearted,
to preach deliverance to the captives, and recovering of
sight to the blind, to set at liberty them that are bruised.

Pied Piper of Love

It's because of Your love, it's because You care, it's because of Your love that You send us to share.

You see them in their addictions and pain, and You say, "Go play your pipe; draw them to Me with sweet sounds of life, comfort, and peace.

Let them know I'm aware. I can see; show them I care. Do this for Me.

Go play your pipe. Tell them they're special, unique individuals, full of potential.

Yes, go tell them they're okay, good enough, man enough, woman enough, okay enough just as they are right now.

So, go play your pipe. Take My heart, My passion. Add to it the sweet aroma of your compassion.

Then stand back. Watch and see how they leave their addictions and pain behind as you lead them to Me.

I am their God, who is merciful, compassionate, and kind."

John 8:7: So when they continued asking him,
he lifted up himself, and said unto them, He that is
without sin among you, let him first cast a stone at her.

Blame Game of Stone Throwing

The devil made me do it; he tempted me to eat.

She said it was good; she said it was sweet. Besides, God, You're the one who gave her to me.

There is a man who lives in a box downtown in Sioux Saint Marie. I've wondered, *how could this happen? How could this be? Could this perhaps happen to you or to me?*

I lost my job and then my wife. The other guy ran that red light. I got ill; I got sick. Now this is my plight. Something tells me it's still not right.

People walk by, assuming to know why. Strolling down the street, looking to the sky—*What a lovely day. I'll just look the other way.*

At night in my box at thirty below, I'm so cold, freezing, like an icicle.

People walk back from the bar, feeling brave and bold. Some even decide to get physical.

They kick and yell at my box; with their friends, they amuse.

When will they realize not even a homeless person deserves to be kicked and abused?

Remember when Jesus wrote in the sand, "You who have never sinned cast the first stone"? You know what happened.

So be careful what you say and do. This cardboard box someday could happen to you.

James 1:3: Knowing this, that the trying
of your faith worketh patience.

Life Is a Process

For every cloud or storm that threatens here below, there comes the sun and its warmth followed by a rainbow.

A mother's pain at giving birth is remarkably quite intense until she catches a glimpse of her gift from heaven sent.

When we suffer a great loss of those we hold dear, the pain seems to linger throughout the year.

There comes a time our pain, through grieving, seems to reach its end.

Fond memories flood our souls; we find ourselves smiling once again as we remember our precious family or dear friend.

No matter what season or plight we may go through, it will indeed pass.

You can be sure of a mountaintop, graduation, or harvest because the storms of our lives never last.

Yes, there is peace in the valley for you, my friend; your faith will always carry you through.

Not too far to go now; just around that bend, there's another mountaintop, waiting there for you.

Acts 26:18: To open their eyes, and to turn them
from darkness to light, and from the power of Satan unto
God, that they may receive forgiveness of sins, and inheritance
among them which are sanctified by faith that is in me.

In Heaven, Forever Young, My Angel Child

No blame; what's done is done.

O the lessons I have learned since I was young.

My early years without the Lord were literally insane, drowning from a broken home in the mire of addiction and pain.

Two hearts collided like a train wreck ready to happen, an intense whirlwind of emotions and passion.

Hoping to end all their childhood pain, they fell into each other's arms again and again.

Yet the hurts never went away.

Seemed addictions and pain were here to stay.

No matter how much they tried to join together by heart, their pain from early years would keep them far apart.

Blinded to the snares of the past that kept them both at bay, their pride fully pointed fingers at each other for the blame.

No one was wrong; neither was right.

The scars were deep that blocked them to unite.

Emerged in addiction clouded with grief, hoping and hoping to find some relief.

Heaven sent the answer; their hopes were heard, wrapped up in love, a gift from above, tiny and small, an angel child with a wakeup call:

"Dear Mom and Dad, please hear my little voice.

God is going to raise me in a place of heaven's choice.

I will be free from all sin, shame, and pain, of all sorrow, stain, and fears.

I will join a cloud of witnesses with all my prayers and cheers, to guide you both to a narrow path, the one that leads you here.

Dear Mom and Dad, please listen to my small voice and see.

Love and forgiveness are the only choice that will lead you here to me.

In God's love, Your eternal child."

Galatians 5:22–23: But the fruit of the Spirit is love, joy, peace, longsuffering, gentleness, goodness, faith, meekness, temperance: against such there is no law.

Who Am I When Life Gives Its Squeeze?

Am I an orange or a lemon? They both look similarly the same.

However, one is sweet; the other is sour, full of bitterness and pain.

When life has you in a vice, what comes out? Is it nasty or nice?

When you're waiting in line or trying to get to work on time and are way behind, are you still patient and kind?

Or do you mumble and grumble underneath your breath, "Why hasn't this lousy line moved yet?"

On your way to work, and there is a grandma or grandpa ahead of you, driving slow taking a stroll, do you slam on your horn and yell and call them a jerk or, better, a troll?

A farmer can be a fig dresser who goes out and slices his figs.

What pours out are all the nasty, sour juices, leaving the fig nice and sweet, good to eat.

When you're sweet, you're patient, gentle, graceful, and kind.

Yet if you're sour, you're angry, bitter, intolerant, and mean all the time.

You decide who you want to be.

Deuteronomy 7:8: But because the Lord loved you, and because he would keep the oath which he had sworn unto your fathers, hath the Lord brought you out with a mighty hand, and redeemed you out of the house of bondmen, from the hand of Pharaoh king of Egypt.

Romans 3:23: For all have sinned, and come short of the glory of God.

Thank God, I've Been Redeemed

I thank God, He's given me the power to refrain and abstain from repeating the past, being an addict full of pain.

You say you've never gone down my path; well, don't mind me if I begin to laugh.

Truth is, you're an addict, too; you've just taken a different avenue.

What profit do you gain by hiding all your pain, striving and striving for more earthly gain?

You've got one, maybe two or three jobs, and you think you're doing all right.

Yet you can't see or hear your children's sobs at night.

All your tittles and prideful grins that try to hide all your pain within will never be enough to hide the stuff you stuff.

So, next time you are tempted to point the finger at someone, remember your own children who cry themselves to sleep at night, feeling like orphans.

If only our children could find the words, what would they say?

"Dear Mom and Dad, please slow down and teach me how to play."

So, let's get together, have a coffee or a tea.

We will learn from the Master that balance is the key.

You see, we are all addicts to various degrees.

Only when we get honest and free can we truly see and thank God, for we've been redeemed.

John 8:36: If the Son therefore shall make
you free, ye shall be free indeed.

Eagles Nesting

Settled, sheltered by the eagles' wings, heart so free, I just want to sing.

Far above all the noise and the raging roars, free as an eagle, my spirit soars.

Close your eyes; just give it a try. Dream a dream, sing, and fly.

When life's burdens are weighing you down, just flap your wings and leave the ground.

No longer earthbound in addiction and pain, rise above, relax your brain, leave it all behind, soar with the eagles, bathe in God's love, and free your mind.

Dream your dream, sing, and fly; just close your eyes, and give it a try.

Nothing or no one can ever hold you down.

You were born to fly and soar, not be earthbound.

We must free ourselves from time to time, leave all our cares and pain behind.

Heed the call to come on up, bask yourself in God's sweet love.

Remember to soar with the eagles again and again.

Closer and closer, we fly toward our heavenly home, our New Jerusalem.

Just flap your wings; it's easy if you try.

You'll begin to sing when you learn to fly.

1 Peter 2:11: Dearly beloved, I beseech you
as strangers and pilgrims, abstain from fleshly
lusts, which war against the soul.

Who Am I

Who am I; what will I be?

If I surrender all and die to me, I will be like Thy Perfect Son, holy and anointed, the Risen One.

Sanctified by His blood, covered in His love, figged from the world and its fleshly desires, undone, unchained from all the mires, free at last, past the past.

The skies are bright and clear.

Holy is Thy presence, Lord; I sense You close and near.

Who am I; what have I become?

I'm a blood-bought child of God, looking more like His Dear Son.

This world is not my home; I'm just passing through. I'm sure to some and most I look like a pilgrim, too.

They rejected my Lord Jesus; it happens to me, too.

Now He's home in heaven; I will be with Him real soon.

So, until my journey ends, I will become more and more like Him, fulfilling our Father's dreams until all have been redeemed.

Ephesians 2:5: Even when we were dead in sins,
hath quickened us together with Christ
(by grace ye are saved).

When I Need Love

I need to be loved when I'm right; I need to be loved when I'm wrong.

I need to be loved when I'm weak; I need to be loved when I'm strong.

Every time we meet, your eyes are soft and sweet.

All I need to know I see through the windows of your soul.

Such amazing love and grace I see, upon the countenance of your face for me

I don't have to do a thing, try, or strive to achieve.

Your mercy and grace are there for free—by faith—for me to receive.

Here in your presence, I'm good enough, man enough, okay enough just as I am, I'm free.

Thank You, Lord, for always loving me.

Romans 8:17: And if children, then heirs; heirs of
God, and joint-heirs with Christ; if so be that we suffer
with him, that we may be also glorified together.

Extended Family

There are places to go for things I need, places to go for a bite to eat, many places to go for things to do, wonderful places to go and see people too.

Special redeemed people crafted by the Master's hand, in his likeness, all unique parts of who I am.

Family I call them—that's right—to whom I have befriended, special parts of who I am united and extended.

Out of all my needs, things to do, and places to go, some of my greatest joys are these, sent from you; they truly mean the most.

They are constantly on my mind, in my prayers all the time.

All part of the Master's plan, they help form me and shape me and make me who I am.

They are mine, and I am theirs, part of your design: united, extended family, heirs of the great divine.

2 Timothy 3:11: Persecutions, afflictions, which came unto me at Antioch, at Iconium, at Lystra; what persecutions I endured: but out of them all the Lord delivered me.

Some Days Diamonds, Some Days Dirt

Christianity is not always easy—however, surely better than the alternative, bondage and slavery.

Anyone can cave and become a slave; most would say that way is the norm.

Takes a warrior with courage to be brave and endure, embrace the storms.

It's not practical for me to live a life of selfishness and sin, striving for temporal gain.

His mercies have shown me how to win and avoid a lot of pain.

The enemy has his tools, trying to lead astray, putting people in bondage, making them his slaves.

A thief he is from morning till night, lying, claiming what's wrong is right.

Our lives tell a different story. We are His blessed redeemed because of His love, His glory for us; for all, He did bleed.

Saved, delivered, healed, we now stand, touched, redeemed by His virtuous hand.

His glory, we now proclaim with grateful hearts, we are not the same.

We willingly help those who resemble where we once were, knowing full well we'd be there still, that's for sure.

Compelled by His mercy, compassion, and grace, we share with passion our treasure to all who seek His face.

1 John 2:15: Love not the world, neither the
things that are in the world. If any man love the
world, the love of the Father is not in him.

1 John 3:17: But whoso hath this world's goods, and seeth his
brother have need, and shutteth up his bowels of compassion
from him, how dwelleth the love of God in him?

Titles or Testimonies

Titles or testimonies: which ones do you pursue?

What amount of money or education will do?

The world says you need this amount or that before you measure up, so back to the books you go, because it's never enough.

Grace is quite the contrary; its origin is from above, found also in our Oxford Dictionary, *unmerited, undeserved love.*

This favor is freely given; no one can earn it or achieve.

God's grace comes from heaven to all who believe.

There's nothing you can do to make Him love you more than He does right now, or anything to make Him love you less.

God's grace is all-sufficient, absolutely the best.

The world will always tell you that you never measure up; even your very best will never be enough.

God's love is unconditional; you're loved and accepted, good enough right now.

You can cease all your efforts and find rest from the plow.

What really matters the most that you really need to know: God's love, like a blanket, surrounds you everywhere you go.

Unconditional, His love is that lasts throughout our day, no matter what we do—work, sleep, or play.

The beauty is you never have to do a thing, prove a thing, or achieve a thing to get it.

God's love is there, like the air; just wrap it around you, like a blanket.

Achieving your education goal, a bachelor's or master's, perhaps your PhD, "Well done," Heavenly Father says. "Well done. Now use it to glorify Me."

So, titles or testimonies—the choice is up to you. For myself, it's simple; only a harvest of souls will do.

2 Peter 2:1: But there were false prophets also among the people, even as there shall be false teachers among you, who privily shall bring in damnable heresies, even denying the Lord that bought them, and bring upon themselves swift destruction.

Hebrews 12,12: Looking unto Jesus the author and finisher of our faith who for the joy that was set before him endured the cross, despising its shame, and is sat down at the right hand of the throne of God.

Living in a War Zone

Cults, counterfeits, and land mines everywhere I go, all trying to seduce my time with the evil seeds they sow.

People on the streets barely getting by with broken dreams I see; they bought into the lie.

Police cars rushing all around, raging sirens in the background, where can we go to find just a little piece of mind? Is there such a place, somewhere safe away from the rat race?

"Come unto me," Jesus says. "This world is not your home. Find rest and peace; be safe from the war zone.

Come unto Me. My arms are open wide. Find shelter in my wings, where it's safe to abide.

In My presence are only love and light. I will refresh you throughout the day and by night.

Come unto Me. I know you are far, far from home. The evidence is clear you're in a war zone.

There is a time for war and a time for peace, a time to lay down the plow and find rest in Me.

Collateral damage, it's all around—no need to go far for it to be found."

"Do your own will," the devil says to them. "God doesn't care. I'll be your friend."

Now they are stuck in the mire, wondering, *how did I get here?* They heard a voice, saying, "Take this choice. Now, welcome to despair!"

We must fight, contend, and do battle. Yes, we are in a war zone. Many are ensnared by the lie; both family and friends, we must fight to bring them home.

Knowing what we must do who are spiritually in shape, the danger is all so real, the challenge is great.

Family and friends, sons and daughters have fallen behind enemy lines; it's time to fight this good fight and contend for the faith, leaving none behind!

The challenge is great, but so is our God.

Let's storm heaven with our prayers, being led by the Holy Ghost, let's summon angelic hosts, from our magnificent God who cares.

Ephesians 2:8: For by grace are ye saved through faith; and that not of yourselves: it is the gift of God.

1 Peter 5:10: But the God of all grace, who hath called us unto his eternal glory by Christ Jesus, after that ye have suffered a while, make you perfect, stablish, and strengthen, settle you.

Full Circle

I was once lowly and despised, a man of no influence, far from being wise. But for the grace of God, ld be there still.

His mercies showed me His perfect will.

Now I co work with His Holy Spirit to help others be restored. This is my calling, what I was created for.

Helping to repair the breach, seeking to restore peace, whether it happens in the short term or the long is never up to me.

The timing is the Lord's; I'm called His "steady eddy."

My heart lives on for this noble task, until all are free at last. So, to this end, I'll press on again and again and again.

I'm called just to be faithful and do my very best.

That's all the Lord expects, and He will take care of the rest.

Like a mindless task, I've done a thousand times before, just put in the time and patience, and leave the rest to the Lord.

Anticipating with such joy yet another harvest time, to hear the Master say someday,

"Well done, you left no man behind."

Luke 15:10: Likewise, I say unto you, there is
joy in the presence of the angels of God
over one sinner that repenteth.

The Jig of Glee

With a godly goal, winning souls, my faith in them makes me smile.

Not very long from now, the enemy will pout, not gloat, just a little while.

I'm certain that these things I can't even see could happen suddenly, quickly, even today.

This is the faith He has given to me.

In just a little while, you'll see, many of His captives set free, here a little, there a little, line upon line; won't be too long before harvest time.

Then I might even do a little jailhouse jig, like someone I once knew named Elvis did.

It might look like I'm drunk, I suppose, but those who know me will say, "He's just high on the Holy Ghost."

Nothing better than seeing a soul set free.

Do a little jig and twist indeed.

The angels even celebrate; they really party down.

Sometimes I think, they tickle my feet and move me all around.

Together we celebrate, another soul no longer lost.

Then we bow to honor the King and thank Him for the cross.

John 3:16: For God so loved the world, that he gave his only begotten Son, that whosoever believeth in him should not perish, but have everlasting life.

Mark 16:15: And he said unto them, go ye into all the world, and preach the gospel to every creature.

"Go Jesus" Song

Just sit right back, and I'll tell you a story about an amazing man.

He called Himself the Son of God, the great I Am, the great I Am.

The world is sinking, and it cannot swim; they're going down by the weight of sin.

Their Father's heart was torn apart; He thought, *what shall I do? what shall I do?*

God said, "I cannot let them drown. I must do something. I must go down.

I'll send My Son, My Only One. He knows what to do; He knows what to do."

So, Jesus came down, and He went around, decided to pick a crew.

He taught them well. Then He sent them out, and they knew what to do; they knew what to do.

If it wasn't for Jesus and His fearless crew, you and I would be lost; the world would be lost.

They went around each town, helping people out, showing the world the love of the Father. That's what they were about; that's what they were about.

If it wasn't for Jesus and His fearless crew, you and I would be doomed; the world would be doomed.

So, I praise Jesus for going around with His wonderful fearless crew.

My heart is free, and I've been found, and I know just what to do. I know what to do.

Yes, I praise Jesus for going around with His wonderful fearless crew.

My heart is free, and I've been found, and I know just what to do. I know what to do.

I pray to God in heaven above that I may be so bold to tell His story of His love. His story must be told; His story must be told, must be told.

1 John 4:11: Beloved, if God so loved us,
we ought also to love one another.

Help Them to See

Let all my life and ambitions be pursuing those who need a touch from Thee.

You're everything they could possibly hope or dream for: salvation, deliverance, healing, and so much more.

Just Your touch is all they need to rise and be free indeed.

The enemy has blinded them, so how can they see?

My prayer is to be a blinding light to the enemy so that Your light and love will shine through; all they need is a glimpse of You.

Yes, I know Your love can open their eyes to see; let Your light and love radiate through me.

It's because Your love, which I know never fails, compels me to do what I do, pursuing those who need a touch from You.

Ephesians 5:20: Giving thanks always for
all things unto God and the Father in the
name of our Lord Jesus Christ.

Psalm 100:4: Enter into his gates with thanksgiving,
and into his courts with praise: be thankful
unto him, and bless his name.

Thank You, Lord

Every breath I take from the moment I'm awake, I thank You, Lord. Thank You.

Every street I walk down, for all the sky I see around, I thank You, Lord. Thank You.

For every place, I go, for every soul I know, thank You, Lord. Thank You.

For those I see struggling, hurting, and sad today, I thank You, Lord. Thank You. How You hear me when I pray.

Thank You, Lord, for giving me life and hope when I had none. You took my hand said, "Rise again. I love you, my son."

Thank You, Lord, for reaching out and touching my life

Thank You, Lord, for alleviating all my strife.

Thank You, Lord, for great peace and removing all my fears.

Thank You, Lord, for comforting me and removing all my tears.

Thank You, Lord, for the food I eat, its tender juices that taste so sweet.

Thank You, Lord, for the friends that I have; how their love for You makes me so glad.

Thank You, Lord, for all the valleys I've gone through. It's beautiful on this mountaintop. I couldn't have done it without you.

Thank You, Lord; You're so beautiful to me. Your love and compassion never cease to amaze. Forever and always, I will give You praise.

In Your presence is where I want to be. It is there, that I'm free, just to be me. Thank You Lord, Thank You.

Romans 1:9: For God is my witness, whom I
serve with my spirit in the gospel of his Son, that without
ceasing I make mention of you always in my prayers.

Always Sunny Days

My world is always sunny even if the skies are gray. The Lord goes before me. His words light up my way.

When I see someone, who appears to be in despair, slow me down Lord to show them that you care.

If they're feeling down and blue and desire to refrain from you, just go away and pray, ask God to send them His sunshine and continue on your day.

Later, when you see them again, they won't appear, so down and blue.

You will know in your heart of hearts that God in heaven, has heard you.

Having a live to give attitude will bring you joy throughout your day.

Your world will be always sunny, even if the skies are gray.

The Son indeed is in you, so let your light so shine, your world is always sunny—actually, all the time.

2 Peter 3:9: The Lord is not slack concerning his promise, as some men count slackness; but is longsuffering to us-ward, not willing any should perish, but that all should come to repentance.

Deep Calls to the Deep

Let all my hopes, expectations be the Father's perfect will for me,

baring my cross to reach a broken world so lost.

Another glorious story told of a once-lost, now-found, saved and happy soul.

Forever reaching, always reaching past the chains of religious preaching, full of mercy, full of grace, with an endless heavenly supply.

Always reaching, forever reaching to touch the emptiness deep inside.

Rich in word, rich in deed, never empty for someone in need, lips well spoken with words of life more precious than gold and endless strife.

Come rest at the well; take the time to refresh yourself.

Slow down and see the calm, still water; let peace and strength consume, filling your heart, now remember just how rich you are;

You have way more than you need. offer someone a coffee or a tea, and plant a little seed.

Then step back and smile while you watch them grow—another glorious story told.

Hebrews 12:2: Looking unto Jesus the author and finisher of our faith; who for the joy that was set before him endured the cross, despising the shame, and is sat down at the right hand of the throne of God.

Every Time

Every time I get up, every time I go and do, I do it all for ministry; I do it all for you.

For the joy set before me, another saved, set-free soul, I'll get up, go, and do until I get old.

No matter what the agony or my ailing grief, the joy of a soul set free gives me great relief.

You are His joy that compelled our great Lord to endure and embrace the cross. You are His reward, no longer lost.

Dear Jesus, anoint my hands and feet. Let my life pour out for them. May my fragrance be so sweet.

So every time I get up, every time I go and do, you know He's thinking of you; you're the apple of His eye.

You're the reason I do ministry, His joy and mine.

Luke 11:4: And forgive us our sins; for we also forgive every one that is indebted to us. And lead us not into temptation; but deliver us from evil.

Matthew 5:38–39, 44: Ye have heard that it hath been said, An eye for an eye, and a tooth for a tooth: But I say unto you, That ye resist not evil: but whosoever shall smite thee on thy right cheek, turn to him the other also. But I say unto you, Love your enemies, bless them that curse you, do good to them that hate you, and pray for them which despitefully use you, and persecute you.

A Former Boxer's Poem

There are no tough guys, only wounded men.

It started way back when someone was influenced to bully them.

This perhaps happened with either verbal or physical abuse; neither one is right or even an excuse.

There are no instant bullies, only wounded men. First, they were victims, their hearts, now afflicted, wounded them.

Soon their defenses began piling up.

Then one day came; they declared, "Enough is enough.

No more victim, it's not for me, it may be better to become a bully."

Then they entered a vicious race—bully–victim, victim–bully.

They were closely the same, both still wounded, full of bitterness and pain.

Then one day, I met a man called the Prince of Peace who put to an end the victim–bully race.

He said, "Enough is enough. Let's call it a truce. Your fight is not with one another. Be free; be loose."

So now, I live not as a victim or a bully. My life is not the same, for I remember those words: "Be free, be loose from all your addictions and pain."

These are the words the Prince of Peace proclaimed:

When the enemy comes, and come he will, he's called the tempter, and that is his name still.

His job is to tempt, to lure you, to argue and fight. Remember neither one is right.

So, stand up and resist with the sword of the Lord, and declare, 'It's not who I am. It's not who I want to be.

You see, I'm not a tough guy. I'm just free to be me.

That's my new song. To beat on my wounded enemies would surely be wrong.

For those who you see still stuck in that vicious race, give them a kind, gentle soft smile from your face."

Look past their captor's dishonest pride that tries to hide all the sorrow, sadness, and sin inside.

Yes, look past his arrogant wall, his evil grin. Just pay it no mind as he gloats and thinks his captives are his.

Be kind, be gentle as a dove. Focus on their pain within.

Walk with the Lord who has compassion and love, for they are His to win.

Between you and the Prince of Peace, with your gentle, encouraging sword, the enemy, who thought his captives were his, now set free and released, will cry, "Bummer,

They belong to the Lord."

Only the Lord God has all power and might, who was and is to come;

who conquered sin, death, hell, and the grave; who delivers them in His sight—no more

captives, no more slaves, just free men to be themselves.

Romans 1:20: For the invisible things of him from the creation of the world are clearly seen, being understood by the things that are made, even his eternal power and Godhead; so that they are without excuse.

You're Everywhere

I see Your breath waving in the trees; I feel Your breath on me, with every breeze.

You're in everyone's smile. I see You in every encouraging word with everything You say, from the youngest child to the oldest saint. Your words always make my day.

With every gentle touch and prayer, your presence reminds me You're right there.

All creation worships and points to You, their only sustaining source, and the birds fly by singing while navigating their course.

In the morning and throughout the day, the trees wave their branches in worship and praise for Your constant, never ceasing, caring and grace.

Lord, for those I see living unselfishly, blessings to their hearts who care more about Your will and others, for these are Your true sons and daughters, peculiar and set apart.

Our lives are not our own; they belong to You.
Use us for Your will, my Lord. Nothing else will do.

Romans 1:5: By whom we have received grace
and apostleship, for obedience to the faith
among all nations, for his name.

My Pleasing Child

From the moment, I'm awake, my soul is Yours to take. Let me shine bright from morning to night.

As this is the day that You have made, I will rejoice. This is my choice to be glad in it.

I'm ready, Lord. I have Your sword. I'm as calm as can be. Your flow from above has filled my heart with Your love, no distance now for me.

You're so faithful. Your mercies fill my cup, Lord. Your life, this love, is more than enough.

Everywhere I go, your hands are reaching out. From the very depths of my being, your words of life speak from my mouth.

My heart is full of peace, as my mind is stayed on You. This life, this love, is all I'll ever need; nothing else will do.

In every trial, test, or storm, your shadowing arms always keep me warm.

So, I press on in faith, knowing the dark and gray will pass.

The answer is coming. The sun will be shining; the storms never last.

At the end of the day, when I finally rest my head, my face can only smile.

As Your presence holds my soul, lying down in bed. You whisper, "Sleep well. Sleep well, my child."

Matthew 13:23: But he that received seed into the
good ground is he that hearth the word, and understandeth
it; which also beareth fruit, and bringeth forth,
some an hundredfold, some sixty, some thirty.

A Gentle Touch

Reach out and touch somebody; go and plant a seed.

Reach out and touch somebody; you have more than you need.

When you see someone, who looks a little out of place, share with them a soft smile on your face.

It will take away their sadness and turn it into gladness.

They'll know there are people out there who really, really care.

Love will lift them up to where they ought to be, out of their despair.

So, remember when you see them, you've got way more than you need.

Give away a free soft smile, and plant a little seed.

Keep in mind throughout your travels along the winding way there's someone around the corner; your soft smile will make their day.

Remember that you have way more than you need.

Share with them a soft smile, and plant a little seed.

That's what God's love is really all about, so give away a soft smile, and help pull them out.

Hosea 4:6: My people are destroyed for a lack of knowledge.

Ephesians 6:10–11: Finally, my brethren, be strong in the Lord, and in the power of his might. Put on the whole armor of God, that ye may be able to stand against the wiles of the devil.

Close the Door;
Keep the Devil Outside

We exchanged the truth for a lie, bit the apple, then ran to hide.

We exchanged our peace for a busy Martha way. (Look, I'm so busy. Can't you read what my titles say?)

We're left bitter and hurt, wondering, asking why.

We were not alert and exchanged the truth for a lie.

Close the door. Keep the devil outside; he's full of counterfeits for you to try.

Don't even look and let death pass by; enough is enough of his evil lies.

Let us repent and return to the Lord.

Be armored up, prayed up, head-up, carrying our sword.

Alert and on guard, sober is me. I'm the Lord's consistent steady eddy. I don't veer to the left or to the right. My focus is on Him; He's always in my sight.

Try as you will, devil, you will only pout and cuss.
My life, my will, is in the Lord's trust.

I'm back where I belong, where I was always meant to be, only now the Lord's vengeance is with me.

Look out, devil; it's time for you to fear and fret. You haven't seen the best of me yet.

I'm coming to destroy your kingdom of counterfeits to set the captives free.

Believe me, devil, you better be in terror, because you're going to see, I'm your worst nightmare!

Ephesians 4:3: Endeavoring to keep the unity
of the Spirit in the bond of peace.

Romans 14:19: Let us therefore follow the things which make
for peace, and things wherewith one may edify another.

The Opposite of Competition
is compassion.

Compete, compete—that's all we ever do. It started way back when we were in school.

My dad's bigger, stronger, smarter, and cooler than yours.
Well, I never knew we were keeping score.
My car's faster, my house is bigger, my puppies cuter, my kitties sweeter.
Competition—okay, it has a time and a place.
However, not everything needs to be a race.
You say you're the king of the castle and I'm the dirty rascal.
So you must be the winner then, and I'm the loser.
That's what happens when we compete.
Whatever happened, then, to mutual respect and being both unique?
Today, I'm just chilling, relaxing, walking in compassion.
Therefore, if you must walk in competition, you're on your own, playing alone;
I hope you don't beat yourself up or knock yourself out.

Philippians 3:13–15: Brethren, I count not myself
to have apprehended: but this one thing I do, forgetting those
things which are behind, and reaching forth unto those things
which are before, I press toward the mark for the prize of
the high calling of God in Christ Jesus. Let us therefore, as
many as be perfect, be thus minded: and if in anything ye
be otherwise minded, God shall reveal even this unto you.

My Hope

Fill me up, and pour me out. That is what Your love is about.

I wish for all to see Your great love, for them through me.

To see themselves through Your eyes of grace, regardless of sin's stain,

knowing through hope and faith they will soon be born again—

what a joyful day—and so

much more as they learn to lean upon the Lord.

Even though the battle rages, we press on, growing leaps and bounds in stages,

like an egg to a soaring eagle in the sky or a cocoon to a blooming butterfly.

No one is born an evangelist soldier, they are built with Gods purpose in mind,

To do his good pleasure, come due season, such as this, is just a matter of time

Although the battle rages and the spiritual forces fight, we move forward, always forward, with the Lord as He leads us to new heights.

Gods purpose is clear his burden is ours, his will is for repentance and revival

His cherished love of mankind his highest creation, is clearly seen throughout the bible

Hoping with a heartfelt cry none would perish, in these last days and troubled times

God sent his only son Jesus as the ark and only hope of mankind's survival.

1 Peter 4:10: As every man hath received the gift, even so minister the same one to another, as good stewards of the manifold grace of God.

The Joy of Giving

Everything belongs to the Lord, on loan to us, not to hold or hoard.

So give it away, put a smile on a face, don't wait; people need your seeds of grace.

So keep on giving, and never give up; all seeds of faith, like bricks, add up.

Soon enough, your hands won't know the amount of love they have sowed.

Not too long, not far from today, because of your consistent acts of grace,

a changed soul will be kneeling in prayer, thanking God for His people who cared—one

more soul for the kingdom built up by love.

Nah, Lord, we can't stop there—nah, not just one, three, four, or seven.

Who's next, Lord, to build up and help populate heaven?

Luke 15:4: What man of you, having a hundred sheep,
if he loses one of them, doth not leave the ninety
and nine in the wilderness, and go after
that which is lost, until he find it?

Free to Fly and Edify

No longer bound to sin, self, and smack, I'm living proof He's brought me through; now I'm free from all that.

Free to fly and edify, reap, water, or sow, that's what I do, always, everywhere I go.

Certain of these things, I've finally found my wings, very happy to say; free to go and do, I take this message to those who don't make waves, who have an ear or two.

Seeing them free with the sword of the Lord, watching their chains disappear, witnessing a birth of their biggest smiles, grins from ear to ear.

Now together we can fly, letting the Spirit winds guide, soaring to and fro, until we touch down in the mission fields with many more seeds to sow.

Sure, and certain, confident, we can truly say, those who have two ears to hear will find their wings someday.

Ephesians 4:1–3: I therefore, the prisoner of the Lord, beseech you that ye walk worthy of the vocation wherewith ye are called, with all lowliness and meekness, with longsuffering, forbearing one another in love; Endeavoring to keep the unity of the Spirit in the bond of peace.

Church Unity: My Hope, My Passion

Church unity—let it spread. Put all pride, competition aside, anything that tries to split and divide. Let it go, put it to rest, give it a funeral, let it be dead.

Have you ever heard of *Celebrate Recovery?* It's a wonderful place where people come together, not to compete or race.

They come together from all parts of the land just in one accord. With a song in their hearts, they come and join hands as they give honor, praise, and glory to the Lord.

It doesn't matter which church they come from—be it a Baptist, Catholic, Pentecostal, Seventh-day Adventist, or United church.

Hum, hey, I like that sound:

The Lord God Almighty, He's their common ground.

Here, we leave our petty differences at the door; for me, and I hope for you, we're just here to praise the Lord.

Here is where we have been led. Drawn together as one, we come. With joy, we celebrate our unity, no longer apart, as the unseen staff of the Great Shepherd unites all our hearts.

Now united we stand, together with the band, we celebrate Jesus's victory and make a joyful sound.

Together in this place, with smiles on our face, we sense we are standing on holy ground.

You see, it doesn't matter to me what church you come from if Jesus is your Lord, you're my brother, sister, father, mother; we're all in one accord.

This is the reason the Lord suffered and died: that we would come together as one and be unified.

It doesn't matter to me which day is your Sabbath; to me, they're all the same. I'm not into religion; I'm in a relationship with Jesus, and holy is His name.

That's why every day is Sabbath and there is no difference to me. Sabbath isn't just one day a week, or even twice a year;

Sabbath is a holy daily walk with Jesus, 365 days on your calendar.

That's a relationship, that's how it must be, for Jesus is the air that I breathe, the breath of my life, the beat of my heart, and this I know: we're never apart.

So I thank God for CR and for you, as we come unified together as one.

We are all part of his body under the head and Lordship of Gods son.

I'm here not to compete or compare, that sounds like too much drama for me

We're here to celebrate the Lord's finished victory; as one, this is the way a unified body of believers ought to be.

Forsake not the fellowship of the brethren. I remember the Lord once said, "Never be too long apart."

This statement wasn't meant to stay in our heads; its purpose was to reach deep into our hearts.

Here at CR, I can't wait to see, all my significant other parts, this unity I know, He cherishes so, fulfills his happy heart.

Yes, I'm so glad you're here; you help light up my life—your smiles, the light on your faces, the twinkle in your eyes when you raise your hands to the Lord Most High.

Yes, you encourage my heart. I'm so glad we're together, no longer apart.

Thank you for loving the Lord with all your hearts and giving Him your very best,

for surely, and truly He deserves nothing less.

Matthew 11:28: Come unto me, all ye that labor
and are heavy laden, and I will give you rest.

Amazing Love, Such Wonderful Grace

Welcome, neighbor, both near and far, short or tall, welcome to all, whoever you are.

There is room at the table with plenty to eat.

I don't care what you have done or where you have been.
Just come as you are, dine as my guest; hope you enjoy yourselves and find rest.

Together, let us celebrate life; in this wonderful place, we are all one big family, part of the human race.

Know that you're the apple of my eye, the beat of my heart. I'm so glad we have come together and are no longer apart.

You're all on a journey of this thing called life; here, there are no labels of class, status, or strife.

So relax, be at peace; come, let us laugh, let us dine, equally loved as my family, unique, special, and divine.

Now that you are fed, strengthened and able, full of life, and at peace, go out and invite others for supper; there's room at My table for more next week.

Matthew 28:19–20: Go ye therefore, and teach
all nations, baptizing them in the name of the Father, and of
the Son, and of the Holy Ghost: Teaching them to observe
all things whatsoever I have commanded you: and, lo, I am
with you always, even unto the end of the world. Amen.

Matthew 9:37: Then said to his disciples, The harvest
truly is plenteous, but the laborer's are few.

Many Mission Fields

Mission fields are just a stone's throw away, yet many souls remain unsaved.

Many are addicted, infected in fleshly, worldly pursuits, leading them to deeper bondage far, far from You.

How can they ever rise from their dungeons of pain and the devil's lies?

We, your redeemed, who are called by your name, we are the ones with your sword who will break their chains.

Sounds like a plan, something we all should do, yet who will stand? The laborers are few.

How can this be so? Why does the church refuse to go?

Are we that comfortable? Could we be ill? Not to obey, we get sicker still.

It's clear to see for those who have spiritual eyes the world is drowning in all the counterfeit lies, yet so is the church as she waves good-bye.

So who will rise with me and follow, destroying the lies that hold people in sorrow?

We either rise together now, in our hometowns, or the world and most of the church are going to drown.

He is the vine, and we are His branches; it's time to rise and stop the enemy's advances.

Now is the time to branch out and stop residing in our comfort house.

For those who are mature, already involved, doing what you can do, obviously, this poem is not for you.

For those who are struggling in addiction and pain, likewise the same.

For those who have prayed and asked God for help, please, please never give up.

There are some who know what to do; they are building more disciples who heed the Spirit's call and are coming soon to You.

Forgive us for the delay; I know Your prayers are long, long overdue.

Our hope is for those who are called by His name to learn to obey, and the laborers will be many and not merely a few.

Luke 10:33–34: But a certain Samaritan, as he journeyed, came where he was: and when he saw him, he had compassion on him, and went to him, and bound up his wounds, pouring in oil and wine, and set him on his own beast, and brought him to an Inn, and took care of him.

Fisherman's Prayer

Lord, help me pull them out; that's what Your love is all about.

Help me show them You care by lifting them up in prayer.

More of Your love and power, it's so needed, Lord, every hour.

So many snagged, stuck in sin, addictions, and pain, they just need Your touch to be made whole again.

Lord, take my hands, my feet. Help me pull them out; that's what Your love is all about.

So much sadness, darkness, misery, and pain, use us to reach out; guide them back to Your light and love again.

Lord, I don't know how long they can endure or how long they can cope.

I remember when I was at the end of myself and I had no hope, You reached in, touched my life with Your amazing love.

You showed me You cared, pulled me out of all my despair, and baptized me with your dove

Thank You, Lord, for being there; help us be there in their time of need, at least for them a prayer or to plant a seed.

Thank You, Lord, for giving them Your touch; I know it means to them so much.

Thank You, Lord, for using me to help pull them out; that's what Your love is all about.

Matthew 22:37: Jesus said unto him, Thou shalt
love the Lord thy God with all thy heart, and
with all thy soul, and with all thy mind.

You're My Everything

Lord, help me remember and never forget how mighty and powerful You were the day we met.

Your might and power snapped off my chains, and I was free, born again.

I know by faith Your sovereign power has never changed.

You're always and forever Jesus, yesterday, today the same.

So help me, Lord, yield and pray with my first fruits of the day.

As I yearn for Your presence—such an abundant source,

You pour out Your Spirit to navigate my course, for You know Your Plans You have for me each day:
divine appointments as You lead the way, plans to prosper and grant me health, words of wisdom with so much wealth.

I lack nothing for all to see as You shower down Your blessings upon me.

You've given me so much I must give it away; such joy there is in making someone's day.

Finding myself smiling all day long, I can't help but hum my favorite songs.

I love to worship You, my beloved King, so You know You're my everything.

Ephesians 6:12: For we wrestle not against flesh
and blood, but against principalities, against powers,
against the rulers of the darkness of this world,
against spiritual wickedness in high places.

John 16:33: These things I have spoken unto you, that in me
ye might have peace. In the world ye shall have tribulation:
but be of good cheer; I have overcome the world.

Warriors Reconcile: Call to Healing and Freedom

There is a call coming to a place or town near you.

It's a call to repentance—a letting go, turning from, and turning to.

This call is for the humble, honest of heart who want a change.

Those who come for help, who heed the call, will never be the same.

Here, you'll meet the Prince of Peace, the mighty Lord of all who wants to set you free.

If you bring to Him honestly all your sins, addictions, and pain,

He will wave His gentle sword, cut off all your chains, and you'll be free, indeed.

There's just one catch: this new incredible freedom is not just for you.

Now, you will be a commissioned soldier warrior to share this freedom with others too.

This call is not for the faint of heart who have established evil plans, who don't want change, who love darkness and sin, who think Christianity is for cream puffs.

Think again, my friend.

It takes a warrior to live above the hell on the streets, over all the darkness, addictions, and pain.

Only a warrior can live above all the negative, discouraging elements in the world and on TV, so very bleak.

It takes a warrior to live above, stay true, and grieve through the death of loved ones without a retreat.

To be a Christian warrior soldier is not for the faint and weak.

A warrior is a quality man of God; he lives above, head over heels, over sin and darkness that surround.

The warrior man walks in faith and victory and carries a mighty sword until his last breath or the trumpet sounds.

So until that day comes—and come it will, my friend—remember a Christian is a warrior who endures to the end.

Keep praying for the prodigals, and please never ever give up; always do.

For when they have had enough of their captors' pig stew, they'll come back with a vengeance, as warriors too.

God's calling His army of warriors together, and I believe it's happening now.

They're coming together as one.

As the warriors of light join hands to unite, fearless to fight, for the Lord is their might.

For such a time as this, mighty moving act of God, a rising as one, in unity, as his church finds her voice, is led by Gods Great Son the Fathers rightful choice.

During this time, and I believe even now, there's a stirring and shaking going on in the enemy's layers of darkness below.

God's armies are rising with passion, a flame in their hearts, a boldness the world has never seen or known.

Yes, the army of hell is in terror. There's a shaking going on; hell, is on the run, beginning their retreat.

The brightness of Gods Light and aluminizing army is spelling their defeat.

Their captors have no time to stand; they're too busy on the run, leaving behind their captives, the sons of man, more spoils, for Gods son

Now God's warriors of love, led by the Lord above, are marching through this land with a call for freedom, a call for healing, more spoils for the Lamb.

For every town, God's army marches through, repentance and redemption take their places, captives now free, the Father dream, the joy on His warriors faces.

1 Thessalonians 4:4: That every one of you should know
how to possess his vessel in sanctification and honor.

Eternal Ethics

Eternal ethics: there is only one kind, hearts that have others first in mind.

Their Father's agenda—that's all they can see, pursuing His will with words and deeds.

These labors of love, none can compare, sent from above to those who care, washed in His blood, no longer numb, redeeming the times so others may come.

In their deeds and endeavors, they gently pursue, sharing the hope and the message of God's love to you.

Enduring much suffering, indifference, a lot of ill will, they press on in His passion for many still.

These are the ones who love Him the most, co-working with the saints and angelic Host.

With their eyes on the prize, they embrace hardship, pain, and toil, knowing full well it may cost them their lives to gain their greatest spoil.

Yes, you are the great prize, heaven's eternal reward, no longer lost, now found, belonging to the Lord.

Psalm 86:5: For thou, Lord, art good, and ready to forgive; and plenteous in mercy unto all them that call upon thee.

Psalm 86:15: But thou, O Lord, art a God full of compassion, and gracious, longsuffering, and plenteous in mercy and truth.

Mercy Flows Like a Steadfast Rain

"Awake, awake," I hear a quiet voice say, "for there are many lives who need a touch today.

My mercy and grace—how they flow like a gentle sprinkle from the skies, for you are My beacon of hope, the twinkle I put in your eyes.

Many have heavy hearts out there full of worry and despair.

Be My beacon; go take My light. Send the darkness running; send it to flight.

Then they will know just how much I love them, how I truly care, for all the darkness that surrounds them will surely disappear.

So if you see someone who looks a little down, perhaps a bit of a grump, give them one of your smiles; it will cost you nothing, could possibly cheer them up.

If they ask you why you're so cheerful, tell them your source: where you go when you're empty, feeling low, to get filled up.

Let them know about the great hallelujah pump."

2 Peter 3:9: The Lord is not slack concerning his promise, as some men count slackness; but is longsuffering to us-ward, not willing that any should perish, but that all should come to repentance.

Humanity's Sorrow

Broaden my borders; strengthen my sword. The cry for freedom is huge, my Lord.

Stuck in the muck of addiction and pain, unaware their spiritual enemy has them in chains, people are dying.

Life is short; they're going fast.
Integrity and morals are things of the past.

Whatever happened to "In God we trust"? Instead, we follow our addictions and lust.

Desperately trying to seek some relief, we only add to our misery and grief.

These counterfeit idols we seek and pursue take us back to Egypt, so far away from You.

If John the Baptist were here today, he'd cry from the rooftops, "Repent and get saved!"

2 Timothy 3:1: This know also, that in the last day's perilous times shall come. For men, shall be lovers of their own selves, covetous, boasters, proud, blasphemers disobedient to parents, unthankful, unholy, without natural affection, trucebreakers, false accusers, incontinent, fierce, despisers of those that are good.

Matthew 24:37: But as the days of Noah were, so shall also the coming of the Son of man be.

Last Days, Troubled Times

Seek Him while there is still time, while grace can still be found. The sun rises upon the wicked as well as the righteous until that trumpet sounds.

The rain pours down on both the evil and the good.

God's grace still abounds and is clearly understood until that trumpet sounds.

Come that day, and it will come, every knee will bow down; the blood-bought righteous will bow graciously, willingly, while those who chose a life of rebellion and pain will reluctantly do the same.

Then the Great Shepherd will divide His sheep from the goats, forever to be with Him, their beloved Prince of Peace.

Those who mock God and rebel to the end freely choose their fate, for when that trumpet sounds, and come it will, there will be no more time for grace.

So seek Him while there is still time and His amazing grace abounds.

For as sure as the sky is blue, there will be a trumpet sound.

Proverbs 22:24: Make no friendship with an angry
man; and with a furious man thou shalt not go.

James 4:4: Ye adulterers and adulteresses, know ye not
that the friendship of the world is enmity with God?
Whosoever therefore will be a friend of
the world is the enemy of God.

What Is True Friendship to Me?

Friendship: what does it mean to me? It's something I honor, hold dear, as high as dignity. My friends are honorable; they live a repented lifestyle. There is a mutual respect.

Its birth and origins, it must have begun when God reached down to earth and united us with His Son. In their presence, I'm free to be me just as I am I come, with all my fears and failures.

They take me as they find me; there's room for human err. When I look into their eyes, I see only that they care.

Such love unconditional, truly amazing grace, the light of Jesus Himself shines from their face.

We get together to encourage each other's endeavors and to cheer each other on.

When there is sorrow, it's quickly cut in half. As we lend a listening ear, we soon begin to laugh.

Friendship, it must be both ways, always give-and-take, not just one way, or when you want something, then it begins to cause an ache.

Be careful of those one-sided relationships that only take and take and take.

Like bad weeds, they constantly cause strains; they should be severed and replaced.

So remember, true friendships are always give-and-take.

Friends do things together, hang around each other, encourage one another, and build each other up and never tear you down.

These are my friends, who I enjoy to be around. We help each other's joy and self-esteem. That's why my friends are more precious than gold to me.

Psalm 28:3: Draw me not away with the wicked, and
with the workers of iniquity, which speak peace to
their neighbor's, but mischief is in their hearts.

Psalm 55:18: He hath delivered my soul in peace
from the battle that was against me: for
there were many with me.

Inner Peace Within

Everything is well with my soul as I surrender to God's complete control.

The Lord makes all things work together for my good, a promise firm and true, as He said He would.

He makes all things beautiful; He gives me His best in His time.

Whispering, He asks, "I have but one request: I desire all of your life in exchange for mine.

I'll give you My desire, My will, and My dreams to help liberate souls and set the captives free.

You will fulfill them regardless of the enemy's pouts and stubborn crowds, even if they roar real loud.

Steadfast and true, you will not be moved. I'll be right there by your side.

Forced to retreat, leaving their captives behind, we will be there to greet them with our arms stretched wide.

Free at last, forget the past. They will be finally safe and okay. Equip My people to keep the faith and never again become his slaves.

For I know the plans I have for them and you to prosper and give you My very best. All I ask is that you stay true, and I'll take care of the rest!"

Isaiah 40:31: But they that wait upon the Lord shall
renew their strength; they shall mount up with
wings as eagles; they shall run, and not be
weary; and they shall walk, and not faint.

Day Trips, Mini-Retreats

Stuck in the muck, spewing and spinning, bound in pain and addiction, is surely not winning.

Can't compare to the air up there; His aroma of love is found far above, where eagles soar dancing in His grace, desiring more of this sweet embrace.
No longer bound stuck in the muck and the mire, to be found in His presence is my greatest desire.
This divine exchange—none can compare, its currency far richer than the duress down there.
Yes, come on up where the air is fresh; leave behind all that earthly mess.
Once you've had a little taste of such warmth, acceptance, amazing grace, you'll be compelled to tell others too, so when you come again, there will be a few.

As we learn to flap our wings and soar, we will clap with great joy in the presence of our Lord.

Leaving all our cares behind, we enter His great divine—devotional daily day trips, marvelous mini-retreats—where the air up there is fresh and sweet.

Let's take a ride, flap our wings in the sky, practicing for the day when we all fly away and meet our Lord for keeps.

John 15:5: I am the vine, ye are the branches: He that abides in me, and I in him, the same bringeth forth much fruit: for without me ye can do nothing.

Immerged in His Love with Strength from Above

All my strength is gone. I'm powerless, that's for sure.

Yet in Your strength, I press on. In Your power, I endure.

Many times, I'm too weak, so to You, I lean and seek such amazing strength that navigates my course, yet not surprising when I know the Almighty is my source.

So whenever I feel tired (many know just what I mean), I say a little prayer as I begin to lean. His love and strength consume me; His presence fills the air. He stands right beside me, to whom none can compare.

Like a fire is deep within me, ready to ignite, I dress up in His armor, no fear, to stand and fight.

My weapons are not carnal, or Id. need a second wind; they are words of truth and power, from the Spirit deep within.

Now strong in the Lord, in the power of His might, I press forward, always forward, fighting this good fight.

To this end, my invisible friend and I will endure and pursue this race until the trumpet sounds. Then I'm homeward bound and will see Him face-to-face.

John 16:33: These things I have spoken unto you,
that in me ye might have peace. In this world ye shall have
tribulation: but be of good cheer; I have overcome the world.

Matthew 11:28: Come unto me, all ye that labor
and are heavy laden, and I will give you rest.

Where Do You Go When Everyone Says No?

Fighting to survive, trying to stay alive, where do you go when you're feeling low? Some try family, many try the church, many leave feeling much worse.

They come expecting to feel hope only to be told the answer is no.

People try the government, even some friends, and are told no again and again. It's true none of us has it all together; interdependent society is set up to be.
United we can face stormy weather and flow in harmony.

You're my sister and my brother, please share my hand; together, we will find our promised land.

So where do we go when everyone everywhere says no?

We feel so oppressed, neglected, rejected, even scorned; our bodies are weak, tired, depressed, and worn.

Where will we go to find some relief? There is only one answer; it's found at His feet.

"Come to Me," says the Lord, when everyone, the world, has closed the door.

"In Me, you'll find sweetness, comfort, and rest. My yoke is easy; I promise it's the best.

My love and grace are waiting for You. They're there for you to accept.

I will never leave you or reject you when everyone else has left.

In this world, you are sure to be let down; they will leave you high and dry.

Look up for Me, and I'm there always to be found, just a little past the heavens, bright blue sky."

2 Corinthians 2:11: Lest Satan should get
an advantage of us: for we are not ignorant of his devices.

Ephesians 6:10–11: Finally, my brethren, be strong
in the Lord, and in the power of his might. Put
on the whole armor of God, that ye may be able
to stand against the wiles of the devil.

Armored and Equipped

Thank You, Father. Thank You, Jesus. Thank You, Holy Spirit.

Thank You for Your mercies for the times when I've been ignorant.

I lacked the tools and the knowledge I so desperately needed.

Now through Your eyes of mercy, I have finally received it.

I'm more equipped than I've ever been before.

There are times in Your spirit with eagles I do soar.

Soon, I know, there will be a day when I'll fly away and leave this world behind.

So until that day, I'll help equip the saints to walk in Your divine.

It's a holy road You called us to, a process of sanctification.

Let it be told that I'm in You, the Author of my salvation.

Ephesians 2:8–9: For by grace are ye saved through faith; and that not of yourselves: it is the gift of God: Not of works, lest any man should boast.

2 Corinthians 12:9: And he said unto me, My grace is sufficient for thee: for my strength is made perfect in weakness. Most gladly therefore will I rather glory in my infirmities, that the power of Christ may rest upon me.

Boundless Grace, Growth Everywhere

God's love and grace are as deep as the ocean, as wide as the sea.

They're not just a splash pad puddle for you and me.

Since there is so much love and an abundance of grace, who is being deprived that light from your smiling face?

Is it that someone in your family who rubs you the wrong way or the complaining neighbor who never has a nice thing to say?

Is it the guy at work? Everyone calls him a jerk. Perhaps it's the lady at church, the one who always comes in late, who walks around with a frown and says to all her life is great.

Could it be that political party that urges you the wrong way?

Don't forget those bullies who frequent the arcade, how we always cross the street and avoid them like the plague.

Since God's love is truly so deep and so wide, then why, why do we avoid and deprive?

God tells us to love our neighbors (His love we are to sow), yet we build fences bigger and bigger so they never get to know.

It's so easy to stay in our homes among our comfort zones and have love and grace only for them.

God's challenge is for you and me to let Him stretch us like Gumby with His boundless grace and for our enemies to become His friends.

Perhaps we may need a little extra time and effort for this to truly work.

So no matter how tough, we must never give up discovering its worth.

Let's stop building fences and throwing stones at those we hardly even know.

God's boundless oceans of grace are there for others everywhere we go.

No one is a nobody; everyone is a somebody, and we all have a story.

We must take His boundless grace and share it with all for His great glory.

So as we plunge into the depths of others' lives with His wonderful light upon our face, our splash pads will surely have grown, and now, we are many, no longer alone, thanks to His amazing grace.

1 Thessalonians 5:11, 18: Wherefore comfort yourselves together, and edify one another, even as also ye do. In everything give thanks: for this is the will of God in Christ Jesus concerning you.

The Acoustics

Delightful acoustics: such a welcomed treat. If music had a taste, theirs would be sweet.

They play with much passion and quality of heart, each individually, uniquely, knowing their part.

If music had fragrance, an aroma, it would be their sound.

Their unity, harmony, is very rarely found.

Their melody floats as it coasts through the room, filling the entire place.

Observing, I see those who walked in with a touch of gloom only now, I see uplifting smiles on every face.

So acoustics, keep on doing what you do; your purpose and calling are both so clear.

Every town that you go through, heavy hearts begin to disappear.

Thank you, acoustics, for dazzling our ears and moving the souls of the crowd.

I'm sure heaven is smiling, so very proud.

Well done, acoustics; come again soon. We love the privilege of your presence and your glorious tunes.

Deuteronomy 5:16: Honor thy father and thy mother, as the Lord thy God hath commanded thee; that thy days may be prolonged, and that it may go well with thee, in the land which the Lord thy God giveth thee.

Prayer to Honor Father

Dear Dad,

I think I've got a few things figured out.

I know and understand now why you were never around much when I was younger, and I'm no longer mad or angry about it.

You see, the way I see it, you probably wished you could be there more for me as a kid, and now being a little older myself, I can understand your reasons.

In addition, I have considered your childhood and have seen even though you had parents around, you still grew up very much like an orphan.

They were never around for you and neglected you, and you felt hurt and angry over their lack of love toward you as a kid.

You grew up hurt and found ways to deal with your pain by stuffing your pain with booze, gambling, and shallow relationships with women, et cetera.

I call these "pain escape activities." This was how people back then dealt with things.

They didn't have social workers or counselors much back then, and people learned to stuff their stuff rather than deal with it and work it out.

That's real sad, in my opinion, because then you continued to grow up carrying all your pain as a young man.

Eventually, still carrying all this pain, you met my mother, had a couple of kids, but was unable to be there for us like you probably wished you could.

Why? Because when you were little, you were never shown, taught, or given love much.

So now that you were older, still carrying all the pain of your youth, how could you give to us what you were not shown, taught, or given?

I'm sad when I think of you getting so hurt like that when you were little.

I forgive you, Dad, for not being there for me, because you couldn't be.

You were not healed, and I understand now you couldn't give me what you did not have or what was not shown or taught to you.

One wise man said once, "To heal the wounded father or mother within you, you must plunge into your father or mother's history and find a way to empathize with his or her pain."

Dad, I've done that. I understand you and totally forgive you because of this deep insight God gave me.

I'm healed on the inside now. Good news, Dad: you can be too just by asking yourself what your parents' parents were like with them when they were little.

Were they healthy, happy, loving parents who gave lots of love to your parents, or were they absent parents because of their pain?

You see, if your parents were not given or taught much love from their parents, then how could they give it to you?

Hopefully, when you plunge and see them through God's eyes as little children, you too will be able to forgive your parents as I have forgiven both of mine and am healed; praise God.

I love you, Dad. God loves you too, and He gave His Son to forgive us all.

Yes, even our wounded parents. When we forgive our parents, we truly honor them.

When we truly honor them, it comes with a promise from God to live a long life on the earth.

Amen

Matthew 19:19: Honor thy father and thy mother:
and, thou shalt love thy neighbor as thyself.

Prayer to Honor Mother

Dear Mom,

I think I've got a few things figured out.

I know and understand now why you were never around much when I was younger, and I'm no longer mad or angry about it.

You see, the way I see it, you probably wished you could be there more for me as a kid, and now being a little older myself, I can understand your reasons.

In addition, I have considered your childhood and have seen even though you had parents around, you still grew up very much like an orphan.

They were never around for you much and neglected you, and you felt hurt and angry over their lack of love toward you as a kid.

You grew up hurt and found ways to deal with your pain by stuffing your pain with booze, bingo, gambling, and shallow relationships with immature men, et cetera.

I call these "pain escape activities." This was how people back then dealt with things. They didn't have social workers or counselors much back then, and people learned to stuff their stuff rather than deal with it and work it out.

That's real sad, in my opinion, because then you continued to grow up carrying all your pain as a young woman.

Eventually, still carrying all this pain, you met my father, had a couple of kids, but was unable to be there for us like you probably wished you could.

Why? Because when you were little, you were never shown, taught, or given love much.

So now that you were older, still carrying all the pain of your youth, how could you give to us what you were not shown, taught, or given?

I'm sad when I think of you getting so hurt like that when you were little.

I forgive you, Mom, for not being there for me, because you couldn't be.

You were not healed, and I understand now you couldn't give me what you did not have or what was not shown or taught to you.

One wise man said once, "To heal the wounded mother or father within you, you must plunge into your father or mother's history and find a way to empathize with his or her pain."

Mom, I've done that. I understand you and totally forgive you because of this deep insight God gave me.

I'm healed on the inside now. Good news, Mom: you can be too just by asking yourself what your parents' parents were like with them when they were little.

Were they healthy, happy, loving parents who gave lots of love to your parents, or were they absent parents because of their pain and boundedness?

You see, if your parents were not given or taught much love from their parents, then how could they give it to you?

Hopefully, when you plunge and see them through God's eyes as little children, you too will be able to forgive your parents as I have forgiven both of mine and am healed; praise God.

I love you, Mom. God loves you too, and He gave His Son to forgive us all.

Yes, even our wounded parents. When we forgive our parents, we truly honor them.

When we truly honor them, it comes with a promise from God to live a long life on the earth.

Amen

Matthew 3:11: I indeed baptize you with water
unto repentance. But he that cometh after me is mightier
than I, whose shoes I am not worthy to bear: and he
shall baptize you with the Holy Ghost, and with fire.

Prayer of Repentance

I'm sorry, Father, for disappointing You. I'm sorry for where it led me to.

It took me a long time to wake up and see that Your original plan was the best for me.

I'm sorry for hurting those You gave me to love and wasting that precious time.

I hope I can learn to forgive myself and somehow make amends.

My hope is that You will keep me, Lord, until the end of my days.

My prayer is that I may never, never, never again wander away and stray.

So keep me close and by Your side, for the road I'm on is tough.

I know with Your help, strength, and power I can do it; I'll do it for love. God is love.

So everyone you ever loved, with us or in heaven, their love for you cheers you on with so great a cloud of witnesses until that day when we see the Master of Love, and hear His wonderful words well done.

So parents, be proud of your daughters and sons, no matter what career choices they choose to do, even if you disapprove.

God has uniquely and individually given them special gifts, and they and their gifts are a gift to you.

147

God loves sinners yet hates sin because God knows that sin may seem pleasurable at first but leads to addiction, misery, and pain.

Even as parents, we realize we love our children unconditionally; however, we don't like, and disapprove of, their poor behavior, so we try to correct that behavior by disciplining in one form or another, always knowing and separating the poor behavior from our unconditional, undying love for our child.

God is just like a loving parent whose love endures forever and who realizes that you are so much better than your sin. God will always love you but will always chastise and discipline you because He cares and has undying love for you and knows that you can be so much better.
God wants you to be all that you can be, seek Jesus, get free, then soar like the eagles. You can do it!

Remember, your sins do not define; you are an overcomer more than a conqueror, a peculiar person, a royal priesthood, a holy nation!

Romans 12:21: Be not overcome of evil,
but overcome evil with good.

Micah 6:8: He hath shewed thee, O man,
what is good; and what doth the Lord require of thee,
but to do justly, and to love mercy, and
to walk humbly with thy God?

Prayer to the Lord

Less of me, I want the world to see. Less of getting offended when I'm being mistreated.

Less of being defensive when I'm being persecuted.

I don't want to turn away Your love for the unlovely, hurting, wounded souls by walking away to a nicer teller or waitress just so I can be treated better.

Like You said, Lord, the healthy have no need for a physician, and I know You came for and have compassion for the hurting, unhappy, broken, wounded souls in our society.

I realize the mission field is wherever we find ourselves.

We are to love our neighbor as ourselves. Who is our neighbor?

Not just the guy next door or the lady upstairs; they are everywhere.

If you say you have the love of God in your heart and hate, despise, or resent your neighbor, where is the love of God in you?

Whenever I see an ugly person, I'm to see them as You do: as beautiful.

Whenever I see a hateful person, I'm to see them as loving.

Whenever I see an angry person, I'm to realize they are hurting and be moved with Your compassion toward them.

I'm to see no one after the flesh that is in their poor, sinful state or condition but to see them as You do: saved, delivered, healed, redeemed, righteous, holy children of God.

Besides, there I go but by the grace of God.

We are to call these things that are not as though they were.

This gives glory to Your redeeming power, Lord.

Therefore, I need more of Your mercy, grace, and forgiveness for them, Lord.

Why? Because I realize that they are caught, ensnared, bitterly wounded, and held captive in the enemy's camp.

I want them to see more of You, Lord, and a lot less of me.

I know You're not easily offended or defensive; on the contrary, you're full of mercy, grace, compassion, and forgiveness toward them, because You know that they know not what they do.

When the enemy tries to use them to hurt and offend us, because that's usually what wounded people do, he's bent on trying to steal our joy and bring us down.

He knows that if he can succeed at stealing our joy, he can steal our strength.

Let it be a golden opportunity for us to minister the kingdom.

No weapons formed against us shall prosper.

What the enemy means to try to do us harm and steal our joy just becomes a golden opportunity to minister God's love.

Lord, rise in me in the fullness of Your mercy and compassion, and enable me to respond gracefully and compassionately.

You see their fallen condition through the flesh and painful hurts from the past, and I know You are moved, touched, and full of compassion toward them.

Furthermore, you see their potential being free, healed, and redeemed.

You care and love them so much; therefore, Lord, when I'm

tempted to be offended, please pour out Your power of more love, more mercy, more grace and forgiveness.

They need to see *only* You and Your great love for them in me.

Amen

Helpful Resources for Recovery

This segment offers various resources available for finding hope, healing and recovery.

There is a Christian program called Teen Challenge, with many locations throughout the province of Ontario and Canada as a whole. Many are located among peaceful farmlands. Their instructors are experts, helping countless teenagers and older individuals find hope, restoration and healing. This program has an 85 percent success rate of participants of all ages that return to society with a second chance at life. The majority of the clients are there to overcome their substance-abuse issues as well as learn how to restore broken relationships. However, I believe the same principles of recovery apply to someone overcoming a gambling addiction. Likewise, there are many 12-step programs based on Christian principals throughout the United States.

CANADIAN WEBSITE: HTTP://WWW.TEENCHALLENGE.CA
US WEBSITE: HTTP://TEENCHALLENGEUSA.COM

A Christian counsellor qualified in helping those who struggle with addictions is another suggested resource. These skilled professionals are able to help guide someone through the steps to recovery. Some individuals much prefer a private counselling situation over a group setting because it is more personalized care. In fact, many have found their recovery grew in leaps and bounds because of the individual time and attention they received.

Whatever your choice, keep in mind that both have benefits. In a group setting, you can learn from other people's tools and strategies how they deal with overcoming issues and also receive encouragement.

CANADIAN WEBSITE: CROSSROADS HTTP://CROSSROADS.CA

BAYRIDGE FAMILY CENTRE: (905) 319-1488 They have specialized, in blending their faith along with Biblical applied principal skills, providing expert counselling applying cognitive therapy to both youth and adults suffering with addiction grief and loss.

HTTP://WWW.BAYRIDGEFAMILYCENTER.COM

There is another wonderful Christian program that is also very successful at helping men and women overcome addictions, childhood hurts, issues, and bad habits. This group is called Celebrate Recovery, and it is spreading throughout North America. They run groups for recovering from life issues and addictions. Both types of groups are run in a safe, confidential setting, where there is no pressure or judgement. What is shared in the group, stays in the group. Many who attend these groups find great freedom, and they overcome and reduce a lot of their issues and stress. Many discover their true and higher power, Jesus Christ, through this great program. They find more hope and freedom than they ever dreamed was possible. Relationships are restored and new ones forged. Some people stay, and others move on to live healthier, happier, and more productive lives. Most importantly, they discover a much closer, more intimate relationship with the Lord. Another benefit that blossomed, some of their new friendships turn into accountability partners and even sponsors, meeting regularly for coffee and to encourage and support each others progress. The sponsor acts as a coach and at times may try to guide and offer support. When someone is in Celebrate Recovery, it is vitally important to have someone in both of these roles to help prevent relapse.

US WEBSITE: HTTP://WWW.SADDLEBACK.COM

CANADIAN WEBSITE: HTTP://WWW.CELEBRATERECOVERY.CA/CR

Another option is to talk to a pastor of a Bible-believing church. Pastors are equipped to guide you to the most qualified person to help you. Many times pastors can be very busy people attending weddings funerals baptisms, and visiting the sick in hospitals, there for a wise pastor can recognize skills and talents in other members of their body of believers and delegate and use their skills. Others do not necessary have the time or skills as someone who has specialized in say a certain addiction field. Wisdom would not leave those in need stranded or waiting weeks or months to see a Pastor, perhaps leading them to discouragement or even worse. Those who are in a desperate state needing to speak to someone immediately should be able to do so. Coming clean and being brutally honest with yourself and others will lead you to a pathway of peace, help, hope and healing, but honesty is the key. There is an old saying: "You're only as sick as your secrets." It takes humility to admit that your life has become unmanageable and you are in need of help, but God gives favour to those who are humble. It's amazing how many stories I've heard in which people say that once they open up and talk about their issues, they feel much lighter and better. Sometimes, a person is encouraged to be open and honest just by hearing others do so.. It is very freeing to find out that others have the same or similar problems—that you're not the only one who has a certain issue. Soon, the weight from years of carrying deep, dark secrets will lessen as you discover the wonderful grace and mercy of Almighty God.

Finally, you could share your concerns with a trustworthy, nonjudgmental friend who doesn't struggle with the same issues as you do. Perhaps you could develop a new hobby with him or her or learn one of their hobbies that is healthier than gambling. There are many creative activities that don't involve competition. It is important to avoid putting yourself in a position where you could suffer loss. No one really likes to lose, and not everybody is built to lose gracefully. In fact, most of us get angry if we lose something we value, such as a job or driver's license. There are, however, countless creative, free, fun things to do. Choosing to explore new avenues and environments or relationships can create a consistent flow of happy, peaceful emotions, which are free from anger and loss. This is called substitution. Gambling and other addictions are a universal problem in this fallen world that we are temporarily living in. Remember, heaven is full of former drunkards, murderers, prostitutes, liars, thieves, and adulterous people who have all been washed by the blood of the lamb to get there. It's okay to admit that we have issues and problems. Overcoming them makes us stronger people who are more empathetic and compassionate.

> Romans 11-31 Even so these also have now been
> disobedient, that through the mercy shown you they
> also may obtain mercy.

God will never waste a time we get hurt. The pain we endure becomes our teacher and allows us to connect with others.

If you or someone you know is suffering with any addiction, you need not suffer alone, a problem shared is a problem cut in half. If you recommend this book to someone, they can overcome and find hope as others have. We are all called to be over comers, and we can do it through the strength of Christ.

Printed in the United States
By Bookmasters